Piano • Vocal • Guitar

THE SONGS OF
IRVING BERLIN™
BROADWAY SONGS

CONTENTS

Cover Photo: Irving Berlin at the opening of the Paris Theatre, New York, 1948. From the collection of the American Museum of the Moving Image.

ISBN 0-7935-0380-9

Hal Leonard Publishing Corporation
7777 West Bluemound Road P.O. Box 13819 Milwaukee, WI 53213

ANYTHING YOU CAN DO

Words and Music by
IRVING BERLIN

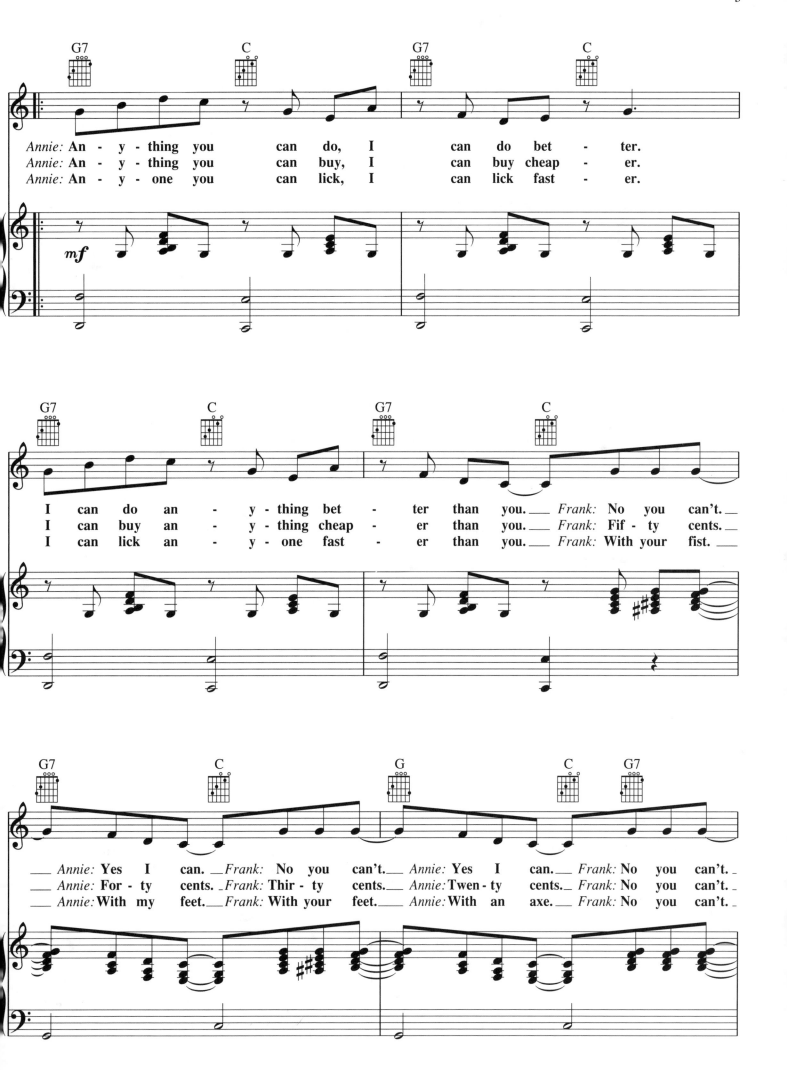

4

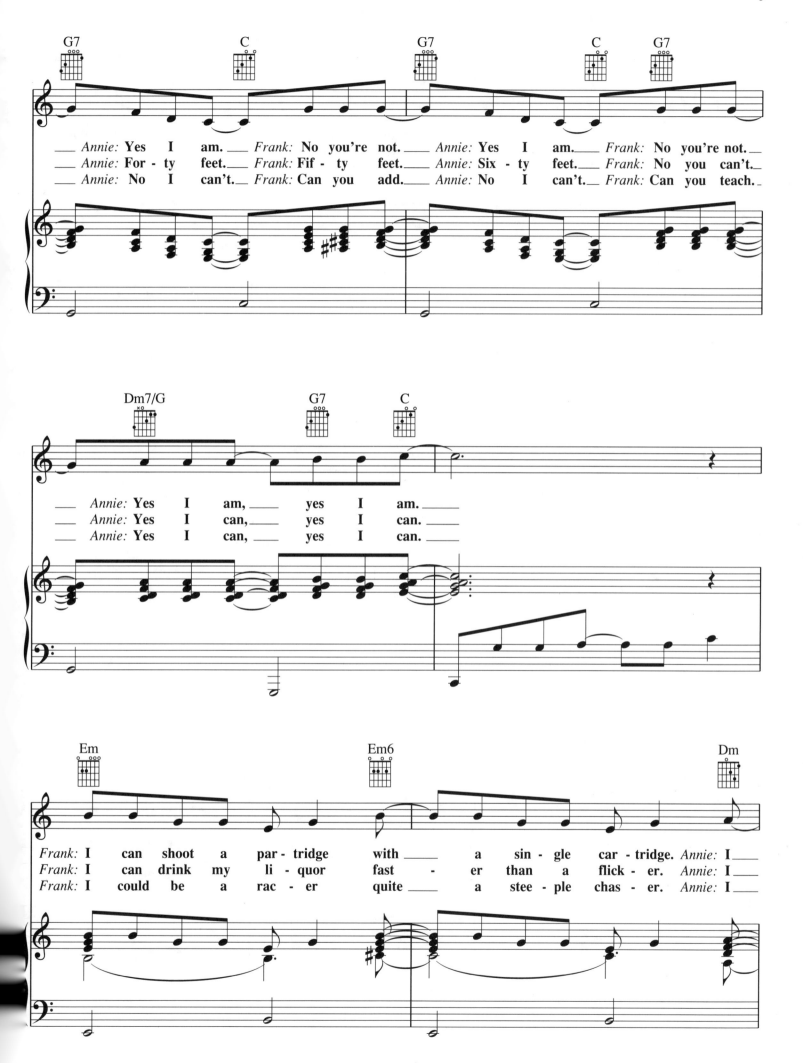

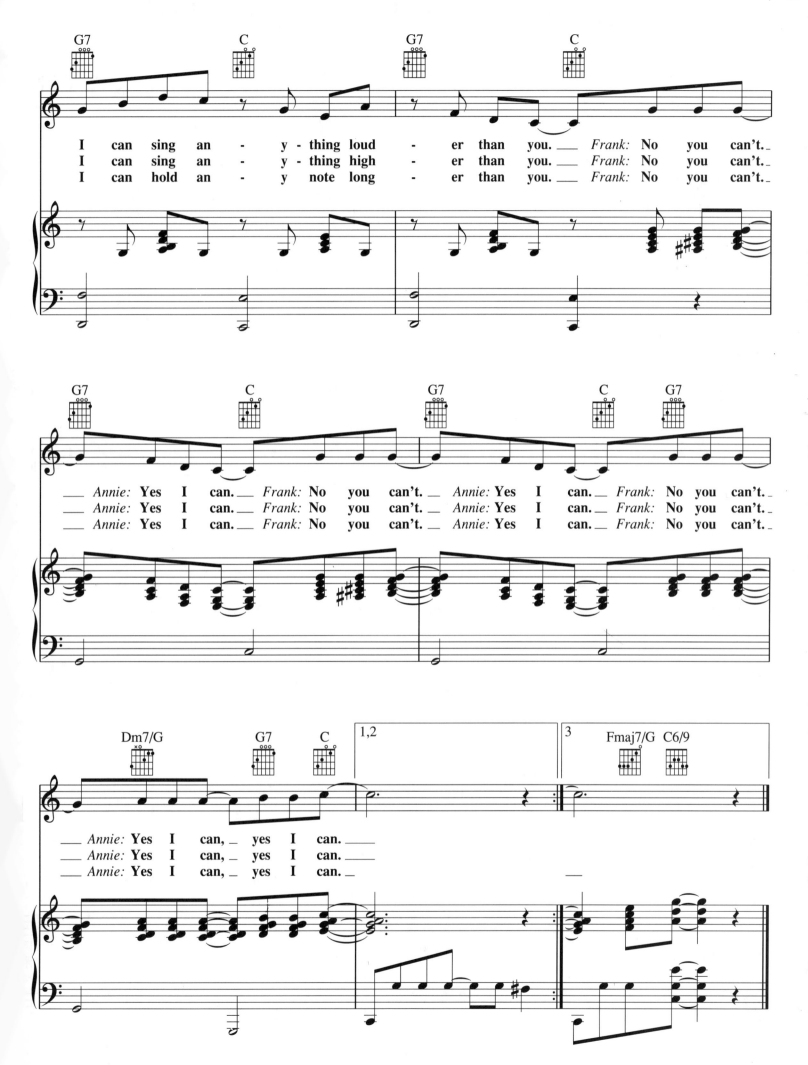

THE BEST THING FOR YOU

Words and Music by
IRVING BERLIN

DOIN' WHAT COMES NATUR'LLY

Words and Music by
IRVING BERLIN

Folks are dumb where I come from. They ain't had an - y
Cou - sin Jack in - sured his shack and now he plays with

learn - in'. Still they're hap - py as can be
match - es. He'll col - lect just wait and see

do - in' what comes nat - ur - 'lly. (Do - in' what comes nat - ur - 'lly.)
do - in' what comes nat - ur - 'lly. (Do - in' what comes nat - ur - 'lly.)

EMPTY POCKETS FILLED WITH LOVE

Words and Music by
IRVING BERLIN

23

HARLEM ON MY MIND

Words and Music by
IRVING BERLIN

I GOT THE SUN IN THE MORNING

Words and Music by
IRVING BERLIN

HEAT WAVE

Words and Music by
IRVING BERLIN

A heat wave blew right in-to town ___ last week. ___ She came from the Is-land of Mar-tin-ique. ___

I LEFT MY HEART AT THE STAGE DOOR CANTEEN

Words and Music by
IRVING BERLIN

Old Mis - ter Ab - sent - mind - ed, that's me. _____ Just as for -

IT'S A LOVELY DAY TODAY

Words and Music by
IRVING BERLIN

It's a love-ly day to-day. ___ So what-ev-er you've got to do, ___ you've got a love-ly day to do it in, ___ that's true. ___ And I

JUST ONE WAY TO SAY "I LOVE YOU"

Words and Music by
IRVING BERLIN

LET'S HAVE ANOTHER CUP OF COFFEE

Words and Music by
IRVING BERLIN

LET'S TAKE AN OLD FASHIONED WALK

Words and Music by
IRVING BERLIN

Bright Waltz tempo

Some coup - les go for a bug - gy ride
I used to go dream of a mil - lion - aire

when they start car - ing a lot.
hand - some and rich from the States.

Oth - ers will bi - cy - cle side by side
Tak - ing me out for a breath of air

57

LITTLE FISH IN A BIG POND

Words and Music by
IRVING BERLIN

MARRYING FOR LOVE

Words and Music by
IRVING BERLIN

AN OLD FASHIONED WEDDING

Words and Music by
IRVING BERLIN

72

A PRETTY GIRL IS LIKE A MELODY

Words and Music by
IRVING BERLIN

I have an ear for mu - sic, and I have an eye for a

maid. _____ I like a pret - ty girl - ie, with

each pret - ty tune that's played. _____ They go to - geth - er,

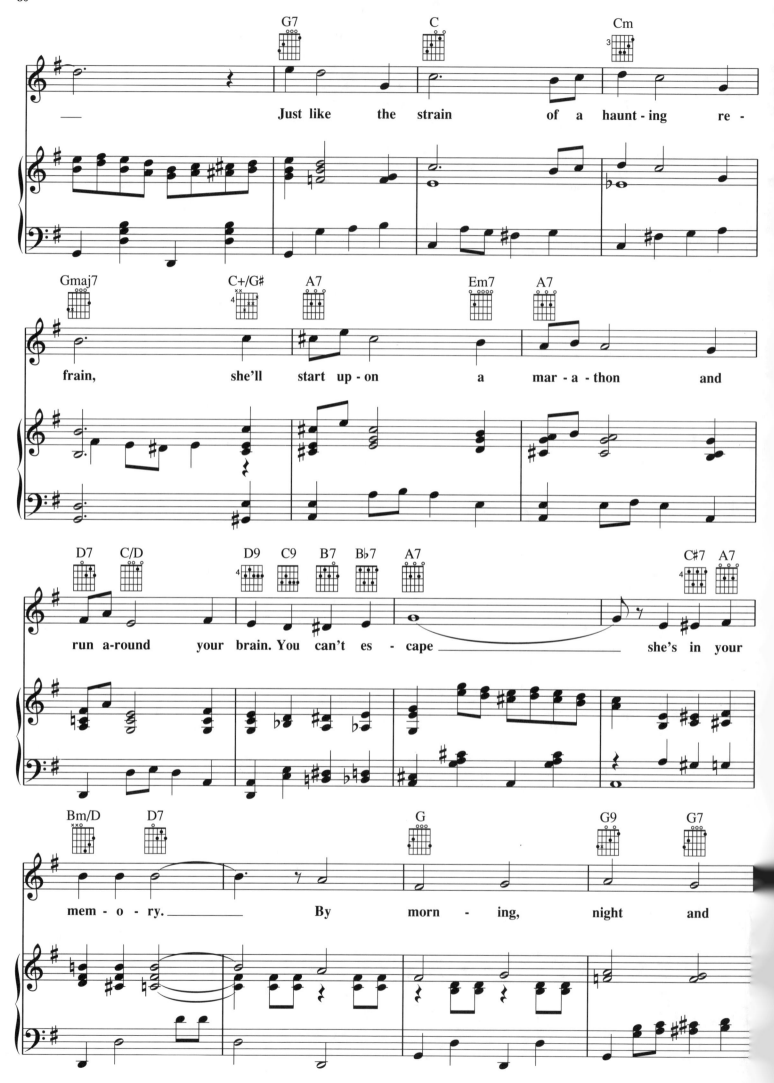

PARIS WAKES UP AND SMILES

Words and Music by
IRVING BERLIN

SHAKING THE BLUES AWAY

Words and Music by
IRVING BERLIN

There's an old su - per-sti - tion

SAY IT WITH MUSIC

Words and Music by
IRVING BERLIN

SOFT LIGHTS AND SWEET MUSIC

Words and Music by
IRVING BERLIN

SUPPER TIME

Words and Music by
IRVING BERLIN

Sup-per time, ___ I should set the ta - ble 'cause it's sup-per time. ___

Some-how I'm not a - ble 'cause that man o' - mine ___ ain't com-in' home ___ no

THERE'S NO BUSINESS LIKE SHOW BUSINESS

Words and Music by
IRVING BERLIN

WHAT CHANCE HAVE I WITH LOVE

Words and Music by
IRVING BERLIN

YOU CAN HAVE HIM

Words and Music by
IRVING BERLIN

(I WONDER WHY?)
YOU'RE JUST IN LOVE

Words and Music by
IRVING BERLIN

why?_____ I won-der why?_____

F

Gm7   Gb7b5

F

I keep toss-ing in my sleep at night.____

F7   Bb

And what's more I've lost my ap - pet - ite.____

Gm   Gm7   C7   F   D7b9

Stars that used to twin-kle in the skies____ are twin-kling

THE WALTZ OF LONG AGO

Words and Music by
IRVING BERLIN